Sidewalk Games

by Glen Vecchione
Illustrated by Blanche Sims

Sterling Publishing Co., Inc.
New York

For Briana and Nicholas Vecchione

Library of Congress Cataloging-in-Publication Data Available

2 4 6 8 10 9 7 5 3 1

Published in paperback in 2005 by Sterling Publishing Co., Inc.
387 Park Avenue South, New York, N.Y. 10016
The text of this edition is based on *World's Best Street &*
Yard Games by Glen Vecchione © 1989
© 2003 by Glen Vecchione
Distributed in Canada by Sterling Publishing
℅ Canadian Manda Group, 165 Dufferin Street
Toronto, Ontario, Canada M6K 3H6
Distributed in Great Britain and Europe by Chris Lloyd
at Orca Book Services, Stanley House, Fleets Lane, Poole BH15 3AJ, England
Distributed in Australia by Capricorn Link (Australia) Pty. Ltd.
P.O. Box 704, Windsor, NSW 2756 Australia

Manufactured in China

Sterling ISBN 1-4027-0289-2 Hardcover
ISBN 1-4027-2240-0 Paperback

Contents

Pick up some chalk, a ball, and maybe a few other things you have around the house, and you have all you need to keep you and your friends entertained for all time!

The sidewalk games in this book are great to play for kids of all ages. There are tag games; circle games; games that have been played for centuries and some new surprises; roughhousing, and wacky games that will keep you laughing.

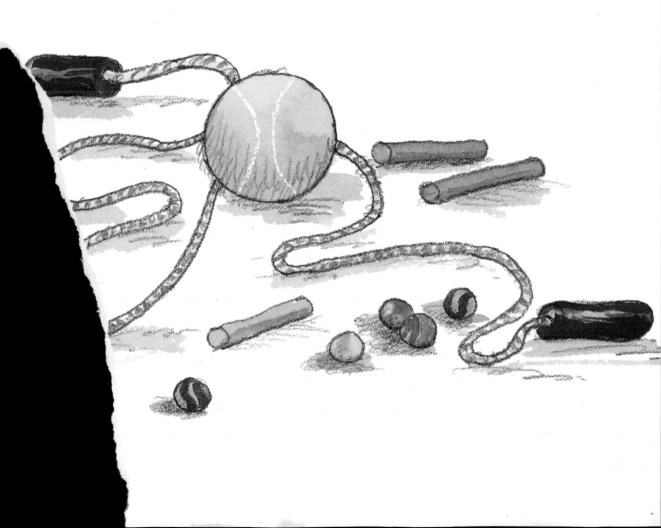

These games used to be played out on the street, when streets were really peaceful and empty most of the time. But streets and sidewalks have gotten busier and are not always easy or safe to play in as they once were.

If you can't find a really quiet sidewalk or street, you can play these games in many other places — such as schoolyards, parks and playgrounds, and backyards, and many of them can even be played on the lawn or in a grassy field.

Have fun with them!

Let's Run

Tag can be very simple or really complicated with teams, bases, and strategies. But the idea is always the same. A player — or a group of players — is chosen to be "It." "It" chases the other players and tags them.

Sometimes a player is "captured" (put in prison or taken out of the game) or that player becomes the new "It."

The game goes on until everyone is captured — or tired out. That's all there is to it — but there are lots of great tag games. Here are some of them!

freeze Tag

7-15 players

"It" chases the other players, trying to tag each one. When players are tagged, they "freeze" — stop right away in whatever position they were in at the very moment they were tagged — and they have to wait to be "unfrozen." The only way to be unfrozen is to be tagged by another player who hasn't been tagged yet. "It" wins if everyone gets frozen. "It" loses if some players are still running around and "It" is just too tired to play anymore.

SPECIAL: An exception to the freeze rule is called "Electricity."

When several frozen players are within touching distance of each other, one of them can call out "Electricity." This means that frozen players can move just enough to link hands. Then, if one of these players is unfrozen, everyone in the chain is free as well.

When the game seems totally lost, "Electricity" can save the day!

Statues

4-10 players

This tag game is a lot like Freeze Tag, but with less running. When players get frozen, they cannot be unfrozen by a running player. The action goes on until all the players are frozen. Then the second part of the game begins.

"It" goes to the frozen players one by one, takes them by the arm, spins them around, and then lets them go. Whatever position the players fall into, they have to hold, like some very weird statues. "It" chooses the most unusual statue to be "It" in the next game.

Sticky Tag

5-10 players

When "It" tags a player, that person becomes the new "It," but with a difference. The new "It" sticks her hand over the part of her body that was tagged. If Nancy was tagged on the shoulder, her hand is stuck to her shoulder and she can't use it to tag someone else. When she tags someone else, she is no longer "It" and she can unstick her hand.

Tip: Try tagging someone on the knee or on the foot!

Squat Tag

5-10 players

In 1559, the Flemish artist Pieter Bruegel the Elder painted children playing "Squat Tag" and other games in his famous "Children's Games" canvas.

"It" cannot tag the players if they are squatting. This makes it pretty tough to get people out. So "It" may have to be a little sneakier than usual — creeping up behind a player — or chasing one player and then turning suddenly and springing on another!

Smugglers

10-20 players (an even number)

You need two teams for this game, the "Ins" and the "Outs." The Ins have a Den, and one member of the Outs has a "jewel"(which can be any object, a key, a stone, a coin), anything small enough to hide in the palm of your hand. No one on the Ins team can know which player has the jewel.

The Ins count to 50 while the Outs move farther and farther away. When the count is over, the Ins yell, "Smugglers!" and they rush out to tag the Outs. As the members of the Out team are tagged, they must open their hands to show whether or not they have the jewel. Of course, the jewel is passed around among team-mates as quickly and secretly as possible.

When the holder of the jewel is tagged, the game is over and the players change sides.

Buzzzz 10-20 players

Divide the players into two teams and draw a long line between them. Team 1 sends a player into Team 2 territory and she tags as many players as she can. While she is tagging them, she must make the sound "Buzzzz" in one long continuous breath — loud enough for everyone to hear. If she can make it back across the line to her own team without running out of breath, the players she tagged are out of the game. But if Team 2 holds her so long — by grabbing her arms or legs or pulling her back — that she runs out of breath, the players she tagged are free and she's out of the game.

Teams take turns sending a player into enemy territory. The first team to wipe out the other team wins.

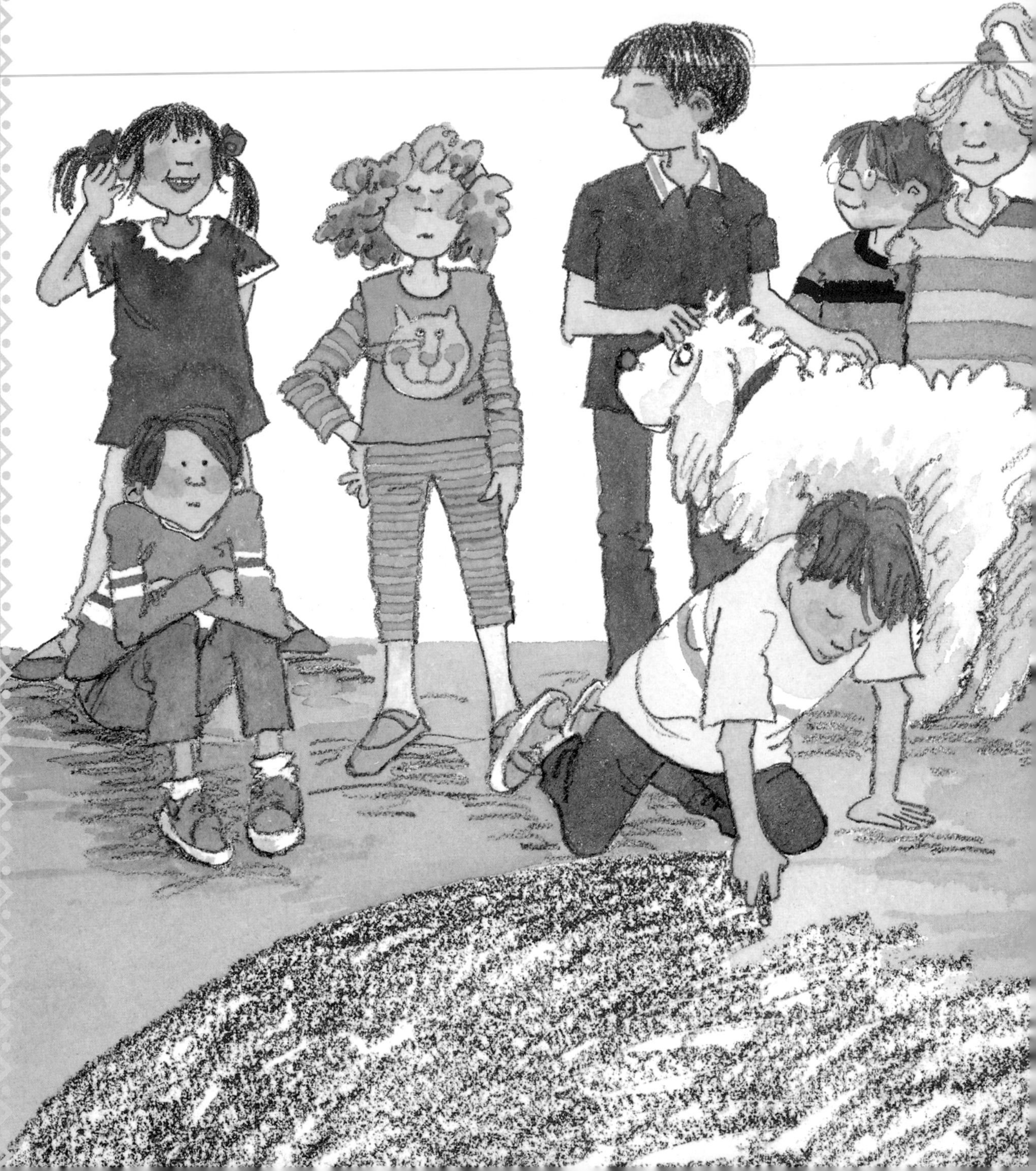

Ringelevio 1-2-3

10-30 players (an even number)

Select two teams and draw a Den that is large enough to hold an entire team. One team goes out while the other, the "It" team, stands beside the Den. One member of the "It" team, the Den Guard, keeps one foot inside the Den at all times.

The "It" team counts to 100, while the Outs run off. When the count is over, the "It" team shouts, "Ready or not, here we come!" and everyone on the team except the Den Guard runs after the others.

The "It" team captures players by holding victims long enough to call out "Ringelevio 1-2-3!" three times. If a victim breaks away before the repetition is completed, he's free.

Victims are put in the Den, where they stay until tagged by a teammate, or until the Den Guard accidentally takes one leg out of the Den or puts feet both in. Players may try to pull the Guard inside or push him out. When all the Outs are captured, the game is over.

Prisoner's Base

10-30 (an even number)

Choose up two teams, A and B, each with its own home base. Mark out a prison for both teams. The members of each team link hands to form a chain that stretches out from their home base. The one farthest from the base of the A team breaks away and runs off. The one farthest from the base of the B team chases him. At the same time, the other A players break off from their chains and the opposite member of the B team chases him.

When a player is tagged, he goes to prison and his captor stands guard. The prisoner is released when a member of his team runs through the prison and tags him. The guard watches for this and may tag any would-be rescuer.

The game is finished when all the members of the first team are captured.

> A version of "Prisoner's Base" is described in Act IV of Shakespeare's *The Merry Wives of Windsor.* The game was so popular in 17th century England that it once interrupted the king's procession to Parliament!

Let's Jump!

Jump Rope Games

1-10 players

Jumping rope is terrific exercise and a great test of skill and coordination. You can jump rope alone or with a partner, using a short store-bought jump rope or some clothesline you cut to about 5 feet (1.5m) long. Or you can jump inside a longer clothesline, turned by two friends.

There are two kinds of jump rope games

The first kind is fancy jumping:

Rock the Cradle. Rock the rope back and forth instead of revolving it. You can do this alone on a short rope, or on a longer rope, letting the turners rock it for you. It's a great way to warm up.

Wind the Clock. While the rope is turning, count from 1 to 12, making a quarter turn clockwise each time. You can do this alone or with two friends turning for you.

Visiting. One player jumps alone turning her own rope. Another player jumps in and faces her, "visiting" for a while, before jumping out again.

Chasing. This involves two turners and at least two jumpers. The first jumper enters, jumps over the rope once, and then rushes out as the second jumper enters, and so on.

Hopping. Two players turn as the jumper rushes in and hops, alternating legs for each turn of the rope. After 10 hops, the jumper runs out and another one jumps in for 10 hops.

Jump Rope Rhymes

Another type of rope-jumping is made up of rhymes, recited by either the turners or the jumpers. There are many of these, but most of them fall into one of the following groups:

Counting Rhymes

These rhymes end with counting to test how long a jumper can keep going. You can chant them alone or have the turners chant them for you. One popular counting rhyme goes like this:

>Fire, fire, house on fire —
>Mrs. Sweeny climbed up higher.
>There she met the Fireman Steve —
>How many kisses did she receive?
>One, two, three, four, five, six. . . .

Alphabet Rhymes

The jumper or turners chant the alphabet at the end of these rhymes. The letter the jumper stumbles on means something very important — usually it's the first initial of her sweetheart's name, whether she knows it or not!

>Strawberry shortcake, cream on top
>Tell me the name of my sweetheart
>A, B, C, D, E . . .

Switching Rhymes

These short rhymes call for the old jumper to move out and a new one to come in. They are usually chanted by the turners.

My mother and your mother
Live across the way,
Every night they have a fight
And this is what they say:
Acka baka soda cracker
Acka baka boo
Acka baka soda cracker
Out goes you!

Double Dutch

In addition to basic jump rope games, there are fancy ways to turn the rope. If you have a very long clothesline, for example, you can double it over. One turner holds both ends, while the other turner wraps the rope around her back, over her forearms, and through her hands. Now you're ready for "Double Dutch."

Here the two ropes are turned toward each other — but carefully — so that they don't hit each other. The result is a kind of eggbeater that leaves the poor jumper wiped out.

French Dutch

Here the ropes are turned away from each other — again, very carefully — with similar results. If that isn't tough enough for you, try both "Double Dutch" and "French Dutch," with a dose of "Hot Pepper." This means turning the ropes as fast as possible, until someone cries "Help!"

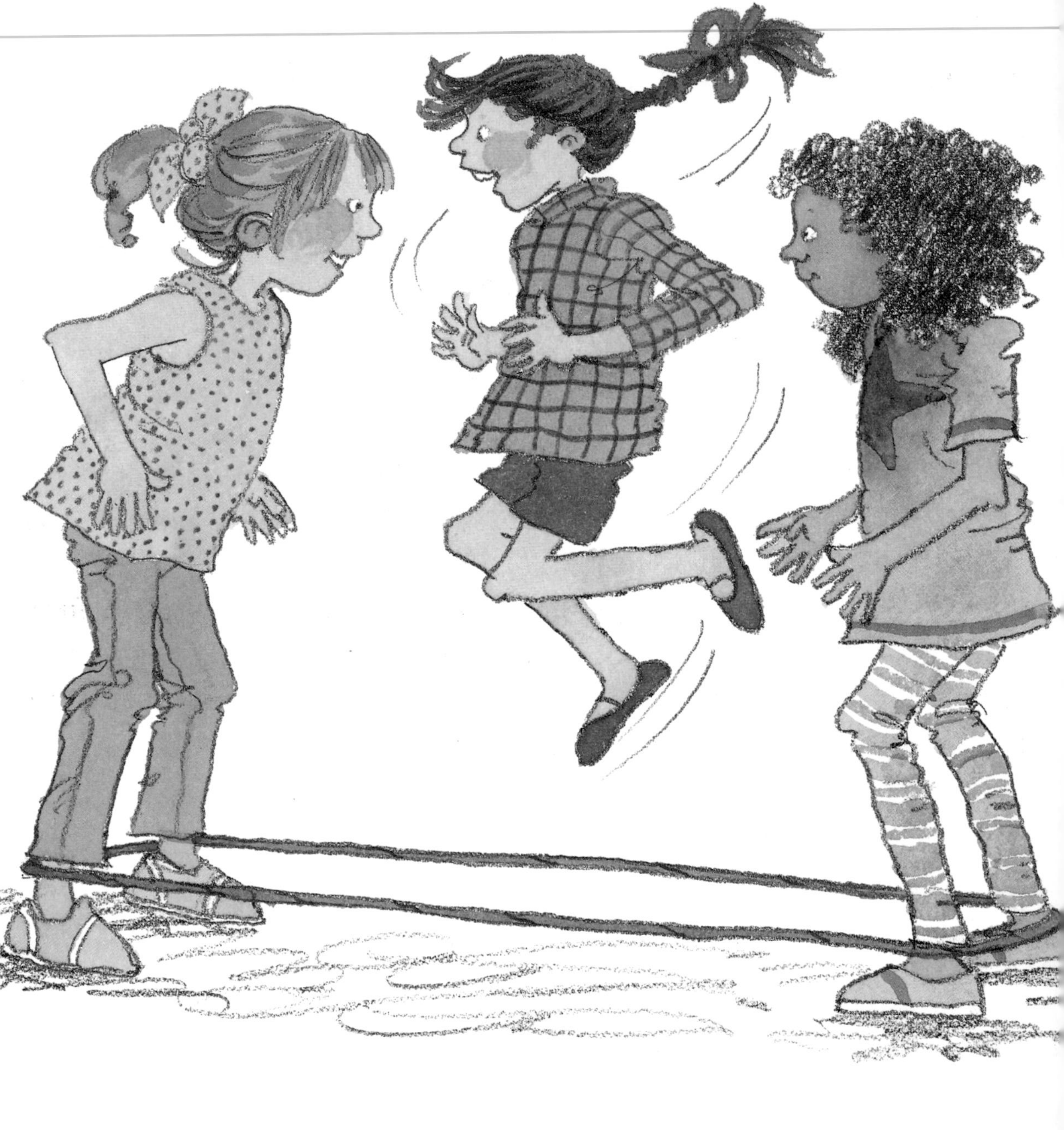

Chinese Jump Rope

4-8 players

A Chinese jump rope is a loop made from braided rubber bands.

Players 1 and 2 face each other with their feet apart and the rope around their ankles. They back away from each other, allowing the rope to stretch and lift off the sidewalk.

Player 3 jumps between them, placing her feet apart. At the same time, Player 1 jumps out, leaving the rope stretched between Players 3 and 2. Soon Player 4 jumps in, taking the place of Player 2.

Now Players 1 and 2 jump back into the rope as Players 3 and 4 jump out. Then Players 3 and 4 switch places with Players 1 and 2 again. Timing is very important. Jumping in and out at exactly the right moment keeps the rope stretched. One mistake and you have a snapped rope or a tripped player!

Let's Play Ball

There are lots of outdoor ball games. Some of them call for two or more players and others may be played alone. Some use pavement alone as a playing surface, while a few require a high wall. If you don't have enough people for a full-scale ball game, or even if you do, these games are great substitutes — fast and fun.

Apartments

6 players

Five players stand against the wall, about five feet (1.5m) apart, separated by chalk lines drawn up the wall. The sixth player, who stands about 30 feet (9m) away, throws the ball at any one of them. Players may twist and duck out of the way, but they may not leave their "apartments," If a player is hit, it's one count against him. Three counts and a player is out of the game. If a player catches the ball, he changes places with the thrower, who has to take on all the counts against him as well. The last remaining player wins.

Square Ball

5 players

Divide the space in front of a wall into five sections, each one about four feet (1.2m) square. If the pavement is divided into squares, let each player take a square.

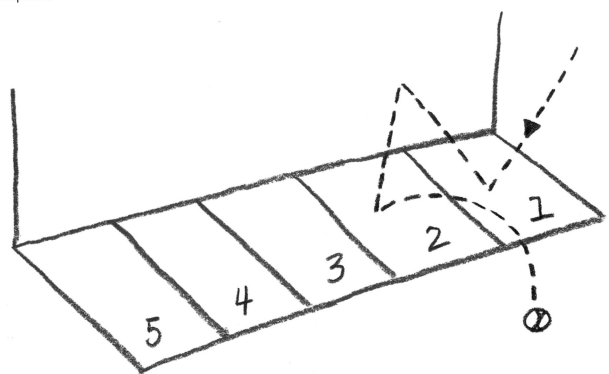

Players stand back about five feet (1.5m) from their squares. The player in Square 1 slams the ball in his own square, so that it bounces up, ricochets against the wall, and bounces in another player's square.

That player must catch the ball and toss it back the same way into someone else's square. When the game gets going there's plenty of running around.

Players who miss a catch or throw the ball without bouncing it first are out, and the remaining players move one square to the right. The last remaining player is the winner.

Kings

5 players

A variation on "Square Ball," "Kings" is played for points. Player 1 stands behind the first square and throws the ball into the square of Player 2, hitting the sidewalk first and then the wall. Player 2 catches the ball, then throws it into the square of Player 3, who throws it into the square of Player 4, and so on. When Player 5 gets the ball, she returns it to Player 4, and the ball continues back and forth.

Any player who fumbles a throw or a catch receives one count against her. Eleven counts take her out of the game and the remaining players move one square to the right. The player who eliminates all the others is the "King."

Monday, Tuesday

7 players

You need a high wall for this game. Each player takes the name of a day of the week. The first player (Sunday) throws the ball against the ground as hard as possible so that it bounces up and rebounds against the wall. At the same time, Sunday shouts out the day-name of another player — Wednesday, let's say — who must catch the ball after the first bounce and send it back in the same way, calling out the day-name of another player.

If Wednesday misses the catch, everyone scatters while Wednesday retrieves the ball and then tags one of the others. The tagged player is the next one to throw the ball against the ground, but the tag counts as a mark against him. Three tags and a player is out. The game continues until only one player is left — the winner.

Seven Up

1 player

Draw a line about five feet (1.5m) from the base of a wall and stand behind it. Throw the ball against the wall and start with "Onesies," which means you must catch it on the fly.

Twosies: let it bounce once in front of the line before you catch it. Repeat.

Threesies: clap before you catch it. Repeat this two more times.

Foursies: catch it after the first bounce. Repeat three times.

Fivesies: clap twice behind you before catching. Repeat four times.

Sixies: do a push-up, jump up and catch the ball after the first bounce. Repeat twice.

Sevensies: clap your hands before and behind you, then catch the ball. Repeat six times.

Each catch counts as one point. If you go all the way from Onesies to Sevensies without a mistake, you've collected 25 points and win, but each miss gives the wall one point. Continue playing until you (or the wall) reaches 25.

Four Square

4 players

You'll need a soccer ball or a basketball for this game, which is lots of fun, especially when the pace heats up and the ball is flying!

With a piece of chalk, draw an area about six feet (1.8m) square and divide it into four equal compartments. A player occupies each square. One player then bounces the ball into a neighboring square. The player in that square catches the ball and bounces it into another square, and so on. You could decide ahead of time to follow a particular sequence — for example, bouncing the ball only to the player on the right, or bouncing it to the right and then diagonally across — or you can decide to let each player choose a target. If any player fails to catch a bounce in his square, the one who tossed it to him scores a point. The first player to reach a score of 21 wins.

Box Baseball

2 players

You play this game across three sidewalk squares like this:

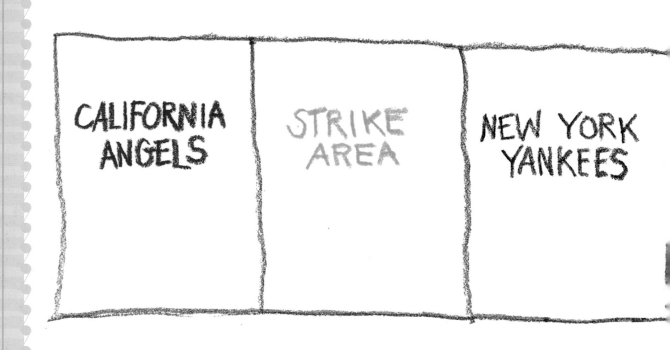

Player 1 is the California Angels and Player 2 the New York Yankees. The Angel throws the ball into the Yankee's box, passing it over the strike area. The Yankee, standing outside her box, tries to catch the ball after one bounce. If she succeeds, it counts as an out for the Angel. But if she doesn't catch the ball after one bounce, each additional bounce means one more base for the Angel. (Two bounces mean a single; three bounces a double; four bounces a triple; and five bounces a home run.) If the Angel's throw bounces in the strike area, or misses the Yankee's box, he must throw again. Three strikes make an out, and it's the Yankee's turn to throw. After nine innings, the team with the higher score wins.

Hit the Coin

2 players

Lay a coin flat on the crack between squares in the sidewalk. Or, with a piece of chalk, draw two boxes, each five feet (1.5m) square, and separate them with a straight line. One player stands in each box. The object is to bounce the ball on the coin, which scores one point. If your ball flips the coin over, you get two points. (Put the coin back on the dividing line in case it is knocked away.) If you miss the coin completely, continue to take turns bouncing the ball until someone scores a hit. The first player to reach a score of 21 wins.

Shoebox Bowling

2-5 players

You need an old shoebox, scissors, crayon, a stone, and seven marbles for this game. Turn the shoebox (without the cover) so that the open top faces the ground and cut seven triangular holes into the side. Each hole should be just wide enough for a marble to pass through. Number the holes from one to seven, but in the order shown below:

Place a stone on top of the box to weigh it down. Now stand back about five feet (1.5m) and take turns bowling marbles into the shoebox. If your marble passes through one of the holes, you score the number of points written above the hole. If you miss the shoebox, or if your marble doesn't go into a hole, you are penalized two points and lose your next turn.

The first player to reach a score of 49 wins the game. If no player reaches a winning score after all players have bowled, collect the marbles from inside the shoebox, pass them out, and play again.

Let's Compete

In these games, players either compete in teams or it's "every player for himself." The object of competition can be anything – a tin can, coin, scarf, sidewalk space, or even another player!

Kick the Can

4-10 players

Draw a circle about 6 feet (2m) in diameter and place an empty tin can in the center. "It" guards the can, while the others stand outside of the circle. One player at a time may rush in and try to kick the can out of the circle. If he succeeds, all players run, except for "It," who must fetch the can, carry it back to the circle, and yell "Freeze!"

"It" then takes a prisoner by calling a player's name. The prisoner enters the circle while "It" exits to touch another frozen player and take him prisoner. While "It" is out, any frozen player can kick the can, and free all prisoners. Then "It" has to fetch the can again, which gives the players time to run again.

If there are no prisoners, a player may make a dash for the circle and — if she gets inside before being tagged by "It" — shout "Home Free!" Then everyone runs into the circle. Last one in is "It" in the next game.

Sardines

5-10 players

This game is Hide and Seek backwards, with a good chase at the end. Pick a home base and one player to be "It," but in this game "It" hides, while the *others* count to 50. When the count is over, the players start searching for "It." But when one of them finds "It," instead of tagging or calling out to the others, he or she joins "It" in the hiding place. This goes on, with the players all crowding into the hiding place, like sardines. When the last player finds the hiding place, everyone jumps out and races for home base. The last player to reach home is "It" in the next game.

Rooster Romp

6-20 (an even number)

In this Mexican favorite, players tuck a handkerchief or scarf under a belt or in a pocket — in a place where it can't be snatched away easily. Players pair off, facing their partners. Then each player grasps his left shoulder with his right hand, hops on his right foot and tries to steal his partner's handkerchief. Partners must always face each other and may never run away. Pushing and bumping is allowed, but if a player drops his arm, or if his foot touches the ground, he is out of the game. If a handkerchief is stolen, its owner out of the game. Winners wait for everyone to finish and then pair off for a final challenge.

Four Corner Upset

5 players

With a piece of chalk, draw four corners, at least 25 feet apart. Then draw a small base on each corner.

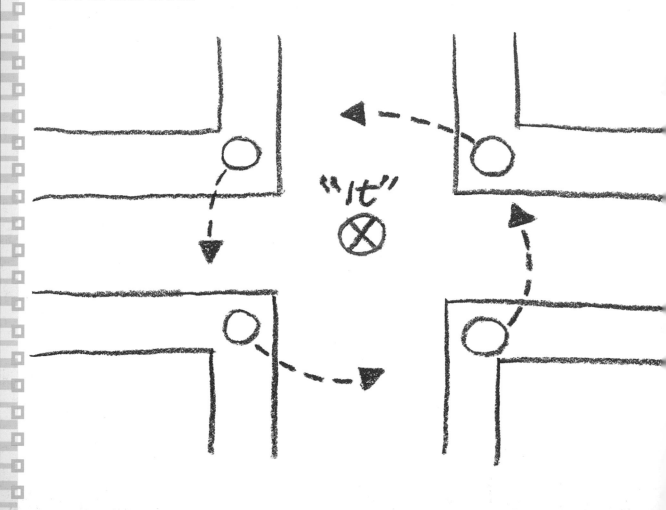

You need five players for this game. Four of them stand on the corner bases while "It" stands in the center. "It" calls out, "I want a corner. Give me *yours!*" and then points to one of the other players. If that player chooses to, he may change places with "It." Usually, though, no one wants to give up a corner, and "It" is forced to say, "I'm upset!" At that moment, each player switches corners with the player to the right. "It" tries to rush in and claim a corner for herself.

It's fun if "It" tries to fool the others into running. She can do this by calling out, "I'm up — side down!" or "I'm up — a tree!" If a player is jittery or not listening carefully, he may run away from his base and find he has no place to go!

Red Light, Green Light

5-10 players

One player — "It" — moves about 15 feet (4.5m) away from the others, who stand in a row behind a starting line.

"It" turns her back to the others and calls "Green Light," at which point the players run toward her. After a few seconds, she calls. "Red Light," which tells the running players they must freeze in position. "It" then whirls around to face the players and tries to catch someone moving. A player who gets caught must go back to the starting line.

Each time "It" turns away and calls, "Green Light," the players run closer. As they close in, "It" usually makes the green lights shorter and the red lights longer, hoping to catch the closest player and send him back to the starting line.

The player who manages to tag "It" becomes "It" in the next game.

Four Coin Toss

3-7 players

With a piece of chalk, draw a circle about six inches (15cm) in diameter. Then draw a starting line about five feet (1.5m) away from it. The players must stand behind this line. Each player has four coins and takes a turn pitching one coin toward the circle. The player coming closest to the center of the circle takes all the other thrown coins and is allowed to take one step closer to the circle. From this new position, he tosses all his coins towards the circle at once, keeping the ones that clearly fall inside. The coins that fall outside the circle are gathered up by the next player, who also takes a step forward before tossing all his coins. Any coins that fall outside the circle are gathered up by the third player, who also takes a step forward, and so on.

Each time a player takes a turn, he steps closer to the circle. Soon all the players surround the circle and no more steps can be taken. But the coin tossing continues until one player wins all the coins.

Cat and Mouse

10-20 players

One player is Mouse. The other players form a circle linking hands and holding them up high enough for Cat and Mouse to pass underneath.

Mouse walks around the outside of the circle. Then suddenly it tags one of the others and rushes away. The player tagged becomes Cat and must chase Mouse as it weaves in and out of the circle, underneath the arms of the other players. Cat must follow Mouse's moves exactly and cannot take shortcuts across the circle.

If Mouse is caught, it joins the others in the circle and Cat becomes the new Mouse.

Duck, Duck, Goose

10-20 players

The players sit in a circle facing in. "It" walks around the outside of the circle, stopping here and there to tap a sitting player and say, "Duck." This often goes on for a while, as "It" waits for his friends to relax so he can catch them off guard.

This animal-name game was played on American farms about a hundred years ago. Like many other circle games, it was played in fields where the tall grass could be flattened into a playing area.

Suddenly "It" taps a player, yells "Goose!" and rushes away. The tagged player must leap up and race around the circle in the opposite direction to get back to his place. That is — unless "It" gets there first!

The player left without a space in the circle becomes "It" in the next round.

The Wolf and the Sheep

10-20 players

Choose one player to be the "Wolf," and another to be the "Sheep." The rest of the players join hands and form a circle around Sheep, protecting it.

Wolf creeps around the outside of the circle and tries to break through while the others do their best to keep him out. Wolf might try crawling under the legs of the defending players, or he may run as fast as he can and throw himself against the line. The other players might bunch up around Sheep or fan out and run around to keep the strongest players circulating. Anything goes, as long as their hands remain linked.

When Wolf breaks through the circle, he grabs Sheep's hand and tries to break out with her. Again, the other players try to prevent this. They may close in tightly around Wolf to separate him from his catch or lift their arms to let Wolf out, and then whip them down before he can pull Sheep through.

If Wolf manages to pull Sheep through the circle, they both join the circle and choose two new players to be Wolf and Sheep.

King of the Ring

4-7 players

Called "Push-Pin" in Shakespeare's time and mentioned in Act IV of *Love's Labours Lost*, "King of the Ring" is still a challenging game of speed and strategy.

Draw a circle about five feet (1.5m) in diameter and stand in the center. As "King," you have to protect yourself against invaders who enter the circle and try to drag you out. Only one invader at a time may enter, and anything goes — pushing, shoving, tripping, lifting up and carrying — whatever! After you've tried to hang on to your kingdom for a while, you'll soon be exhausted enough to *want* out!

If two invaders enter, you may call "Foul!" and take one out of the game. And if three try to gang up on you, you may call "Double foul!" and remove two of them.

Continue playing until everyone has a chance to be King.

Limbo

6-10 players

In Old Jamaica, where this dance-game comes from, it may have been performed to the strains of Calypso music.

Choose two players who will hold opposite ends of a broom or broom handle. Each end should rest on a player's upturned palm, so that the broom will fall to the ground if bumped from below. Start with the broom about chest high.

One by one, the other players walk under the broom, making themselves shorter by stretching their legs apart and bending backwards. To get in the spirit, try doing it while the others clap in rhythm. A player who stumbles or knocks the broom down while going under it, is out.

After the players go under once, the broom holders lower the broom to waist level and the players who are still in the game take turns going under it again. With each repetition the broom gets a little lower until players have to go under on their knees or practically on their backs. Eventually, all players but one are eliminated. That one is the winner.

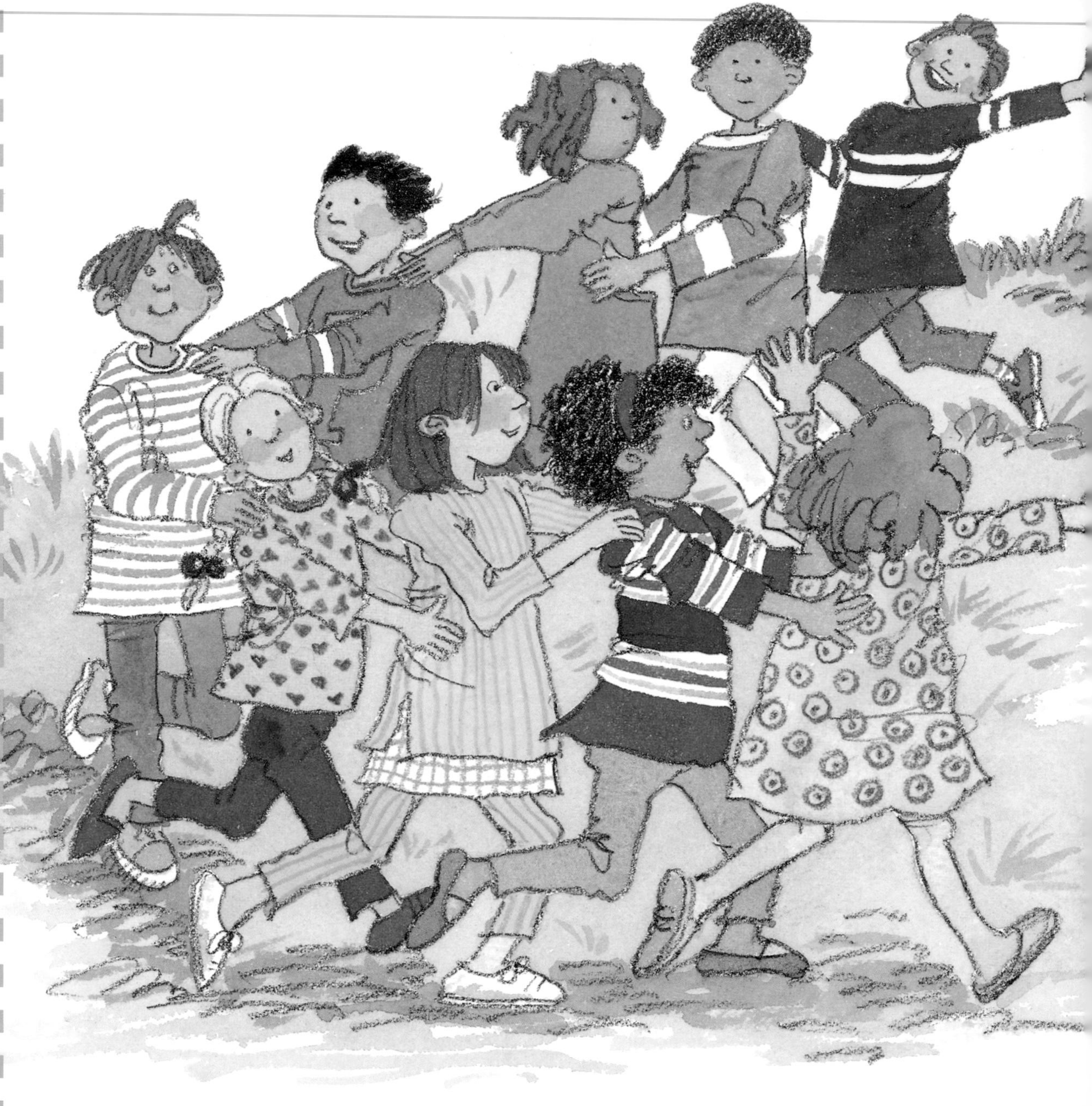

Snake Eats Its Tail

10-30 players

Everyone joins hands, making one long line. Or, if you prefer, you can hold the waist or shoulders of the person in front of you. The idea is that the head of this "Snake" (the first person in line) tries to tag the last player in line, eliminating him. The players in between squirm around, trying to keep head and tail apart.

The game continues until the head of the Snake "swallows" the last morsel of the tail, or until everyone is too dizzy to go on playing.

Coin Pitching

3-6 players

Player 1 throws a coin against the curb or the lower part of a wall. Player 2 pitches one in the same way. If it lands within a handspan (tip of the thumb to the tip of the small finger) of Player 1's coin, Player 2 may claim it for his own. If Player 2's coin is further away than a handspan, Player 3 follows, trying to throw his coin so that he may claim one or both of the coins that are out there. There's no limit to the number of coins you can collect if your coin falls a handspan away.

Continue the game until one player has all the "loot."

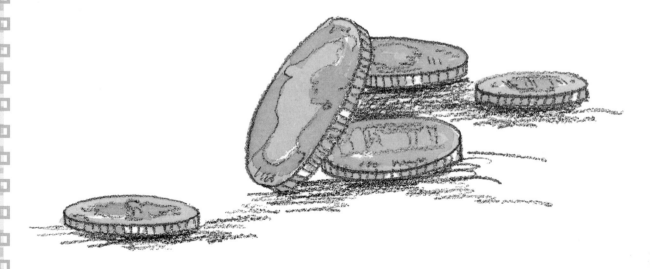

Pigs to Market

2-10 players

You can see a bunch of boys playing a version of "Pigs to Market" in the 1559 painting "Children's Games" by Flemish artist Pieter Bruegel the Elder.

This racing game is tougher than it sounds, especially when you have lots of players zigzagging in a mad dash for the finish line. Each player will need a long stick or broom handle and a plastic soda bottle filled with water – the "Pig."

Players stand beside each other holding their sticks. A pig is placed on its side in front of each player. At the starting signal, the players must push their pigs along quickly with the broomsticks, trying to race in a straight line and keep out of each other's way — easier said than done!

The first player to reach the finish line wins the game.

Crab Race

3-10 players

Players line up behind the starting rope, which is stretched along the ground. But this is no ordinary race, because each player is a "crab." To get in crab position, lie on your back and lift off the ground with your arms and legs tucked beneath you. It's peculiar — you have to look across your chest to see where you're going.

Choose a player to be the referee. He gives the "Go" signal and stands at the finish line (another rope) as the crabs race by — a hysterical sight!

Whirligig

5-10 players

A "whirligig," in this game anyway, is a long piece of rope (at least six feet or 1.8m) with an old shoe tied to the end for weight. One player holds the other end of the rope and spins around so that the rope makes a sweeping circular motion. You'll see that even though the center player is standing, the weighted end of the rope swings close to the ground. The other players jump over the rope as it sweeps past them, and they are eliminated if they stumble. The center player may spin faster, bringing the rope higher. Everyone has to keep up!

Take turns spinning the rope.

Snap the Whip

7-20 players

Everyone lines up, holding hands. The first player in line runs as fast as he can, dragging the others behind him. He tries to "snap the whip" by making lots of sharp turns. Any player who breaks the line is eliminated. The longer the line of players, the wilder the ride — especially for the players at the end!

Play until everyone is tired!

Versions of this game go back hundreds of years. You can see a group of boys having fun with it in Pieter Bruegel's 1559 painting "Children's Games."

Index